D1527115

Gloria Finds Her Voice

Dr. Gloria McDaniel-Hall

Illustrations by Ammar Yaqoub Yahya

A book about the amazing power of great teachers and supportive schools.

Written by Gloria McDaniel-Hall

Illustrated by Ammar Yaqoub Yahya

Book design by Megan Steinke

Published by Gloria McDaniel-Hall

Copyright © 2022 Gloria McDaniel-Hall

To request permissions, contact the publisher at glomc@hotmail.com

Paperback ISBN: 9798408253562

www.urbanlegendspd.com

This book is dedicated to any child who has amazing ideas and talents to share with the world....that means it is dedicated to each and every one of you!

WE DEMAND EQUAL RIGHTS NOW!
WE MARCH FOR INTEGRATED SCHOOLS NOW!
WE DEMAND AN END POLICE BRUTALITY NOW!
WE MARCH FOR FIRST CLASS CITIZENSHIP NOW!
WE MARCH FOR INTEGRATED SCHOOLS NOW!

Prologue

On May 17, 1954, the Supreme Court decided something very important for our country. There was a special case called Brown vs. Board of Education of Topeka, Kansas. They decided that schools that kept children of different races from learning together were not fair. The judges said "Separate cannot be equal." They told all the states that they needed to figure out how to "integrate" their schools. That means children of all colors could finally go to school together and learn with each other.

Some states complied quickly and some other states refused for a long time. Galveston, Texas finally integrated their schools in 1961. Gloria was in kindergarten that year. This is her story.

Before Gloria was five, she didn't know there as a difference between her and other children.

She knew her family members loved her. She lived with her grandparents in Galveston, Texas – she had lots of cousins, like Bessie, Dennis Wayne, and Janice to play with. Gloria was happy and she loved to laugh and play with the friends on her block.

This is the story of how schools changed Gloria's life.

When it was time to go to kindergarten, she was so excited!

She had some new dresses and although she didn't understand why, she found out that she was going to be able to go to the Alamo Elementary School. It was so much closer than the school she was originally going to. It was right down 53rd Street.

It was here, right on 53rd Street in Galveston, that Gloria learned many new messages about herself.

She was treated very badly by some people who yelled mean things as she walked to and from school. Some of them even pushed her. One person kicked her. People said some horrible things. They made her feel like she didn't belong there.

There were only a few Black students at the Alamo School but none of them was in kindergarten but Gloria.

Even though she still can't remember anything about what happened inside that school or inside her classroom, she did learn these things:

She was not wanted there

She was not like the other kids

Her skin was too dark

AND when she tried to say anything, it made everything worse...

So – Gloria stopped talking; she lost her voice.

She really started to believe all those mean things people said to and about her.

At just five years old, her self-concept was formed.

Everyone at home wondered what happened. But because she didn't communicate, nobody could figure it out.

Then when Gloria was seven, her parents moved her to a new city, a new neighborhood in Chicago and a brand new school.

EVERYTHING was different.

Gloria's new neighborhood was called Hyde Park and there were all kinds of people there and these people actually smiled sometimes when she walked by them. She smiled back. It felt good. She actually still lived by 53rd Street, but walking on this street was really different than it had been in Galveston.

Gloria's school was different too.

There were more Black children than just her in her classroom. There were Asian children and White children – all kinds of children.

There was even a boy from South America!

The first amazing thing that happened was that her new teacher, Sister Christella – gently touched her hand and guided Gloria to her seat on her first day there.

Gloria was still really shy and embarrassed too because even though she was seven, she was almost as tall as her new teacher.

Gloria loved Sister Christella from the moment she met her. Her voice was calm and friendly. She made students feel like they could do anything!

Another amazing thing happened during recess.

When they all went outside, Gloria just knew she'd be playing alone, but all the girls came over and invited her to play with them. Lisa Lewis was her first friend. She was so nice and even walked to and from school with Gloria some days. Maybe Sister Christella asked the girls to make her feel welcome – but it didn't matter why it happened. Gloria started to feel really good about school.

Gloria started learning so much.

There were even times that she REALLY wanted to speak up and answer a question. But she never did, even when she was sure her answer was the right one. She did all of her assignments though and she got really great grades. She learned that she could express herself through her writing. Her teachers added really supportive comments on her papers.

Then one day it happened!

It was 7th grade and it was math class (Gloria LOVED math class – especially when they learned algebra). Nobody knew the answer. She was sure it was $2x+5$. She worked it twice in her math notebook. She double-checked the negative and positive signs. GLORIA RAISED HER HAND s-l-o-w-l-y. The teacher thought maybe she needed the bathroom pass. When she said she knew the answer, everyone turned and looked at her in amazement. They had never heard her voice inside the school building.

Then she whispered, "Is it $2x +5$?" Mr. Callahan leaned in to hear her and he proclaimed that she was right. He also said "Nice work Gloria."

Gloria still didn't answer a lot, but she wasn't completely silent in school anymore either.

Her teachers and friends helped her to learn to express herself. They cheered her on. They made her feel supported. *They helped her find her voice.*

Gloria became a 2nd grade teacher when she grew up because of Sister Christella.

She even became a principal and a college professor. She knows that although she went through some tough things, those things probably happened so that she could better understand how important it is to make sure that her students feel safe enough to speak up for themselves. She makes sure all her students feel safe enough to make mistakes too because that's how we learn. She lets her students know that their opinions matter. She teaches them to speak up.

Gloria helps others find their voices.

Epilogue

It is very important that each of us knows how important our voice is. We have the right to have an excellent education. We have the right to speak up when things aren't right and we have the right to be treated fairly in school and in the world.

The way we think about ourselves is developed by the messages we receive from the people around us. But don't let anyone tell you that you are not unique and special. Don't let anyone tell you that you don't belong. Don't let anyone tell you that you aren't beautiful….because you are amazing – JUST THE WAY YOU ARE!

Selective Mutism Info

Selective mutism is an anxiety disorder in which a person is unable to speak in certain social situations such as in a classroom setting. It usually begins in childhood and if not treated can persist into adulthood. This condition can sometimes be misinterpreted as simple shyness because these children are typically mild-mannered and polite. But, if left untreated – this condition can sometimes lead to severe consequences. For example, a student who needs help may not ask for it.

The good news is that with the proper treatment, selective mutism is very treatable. However, you should never force a child to speak. If you are concerned about a child that you know, please seek a comprehensive evaluation from a medical professional.

Website Link: https://www.selectivemutism.org/resources/

I wish a special thanks to my first best friend, Lisa Lewis. She's always been there for me.

"The best and most beautiful things in the world cannot be seen or even touched - they must be felt with the heart."

–Helen Keller

Made in the USA
Monee, IL
13 September 2022

13939897R00019